Shiba Inu
Ryuji

Ryuji Motoshima

☖ 2009.5.13 ♂

Enjoying carefree country living with his lady "wife"
in a village somewhere in Okayama.

Characters

Ryuji
Middle-aged male
shiba inu
Occupation: guard dog

Yome (his "wife")
Ryuji's owner

Paparazzo
Photographer and wife's
daughter

Brother
A fellow who takes him
for walks

A villager
A local dog lover

Ryutaro
Ryuji's predecessor
Occupation: guard dog

Loves

- ♥ Girls
- ♥ Red meat
- ♥ Facial massages
- ♥ Sunflower seeds
- ♥ Bread crusts secretly
  given to him by Yome

Loathes

- ✕ Cosplay
- ✕ Baths
- ✕ Thunder
- ✕ Adult men
- ✕ Scary health food purchased
  by the paparazzo

Contents

Ryuji's House

Ryuji's house is right next to the restaurant run by his "wife." Gainfully employed as a guard dog all year round, Ryuji passes his days in relaxed fashion: digging holes under trees in the garden, taking power naps in his kennel, and checking out passersby.

The arrival of one of his favorite people elicits a huge grin.

14

On hot days, cold days, and rainy days, he takes refuge in the wife's restaurant next door.

Ryuji's Face

Once when feeling very down, I happened to meet Ryuji's eye and saw that he was smiling, and despite the gravity of the situation, found myself smiling too. His expressive face has the ability to lift anyone's spirits. It was out of a desire to show this to someone that I started following Ryuji's facial expressions.

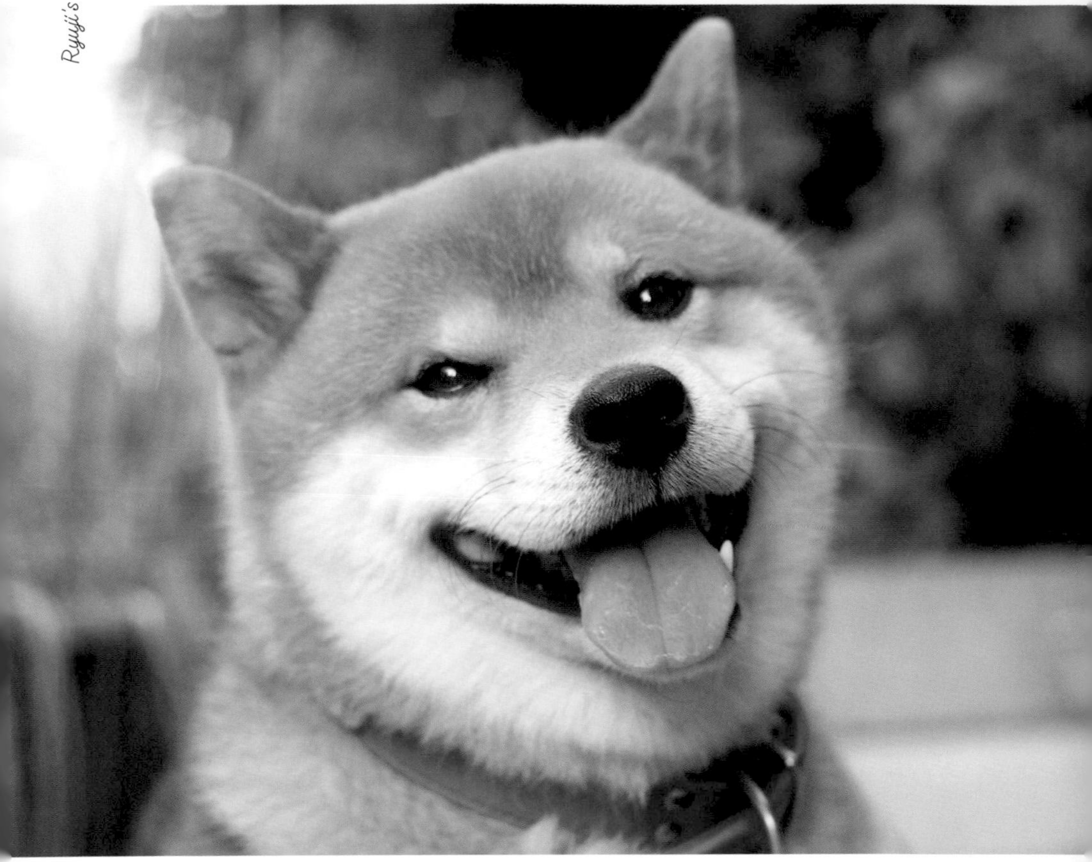

Most of Ryuji's expressions are in just one frame among a series of shots.
I keep the camera handy for those moments when he turns into a canine comedian.

21

Ryuji's Body

Ryuji has always had a thick coat, even for a male shiba inu, and as a result his body is densely covered in hair and as round as a teddy bear's. He has a large face, which combined with his shortish paws means he is frequently mistaken for a young dog, despite actually being an adult—even middle-aged.

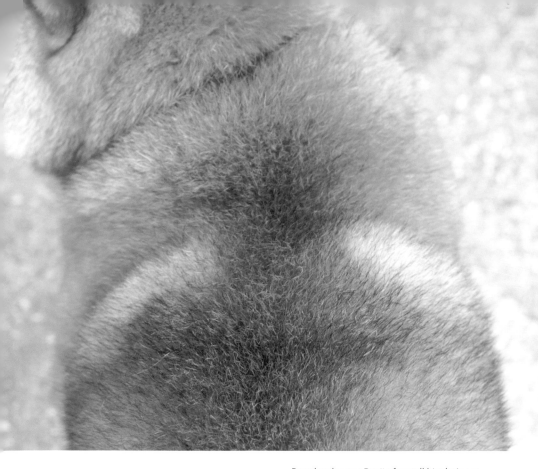

People who see Ryuji often tell him he's out of a dream. Perhaps he does indeed enter their dreams—using the fluttering little wings sprouting out of his furry back.

"I told you not to put that hood on me!"

"Now THAT's a 'Shiba drill'!"

"No one can beat a Japanese dog once he has a towel round its neck!"

"Oops! Caught in the act . . . !"

"Ha! A little rain doesn't bother a tough guy like me!"

"A thoughtful expression, but likely thinking very little."

"Come on, entertain me."

"Please brush me hard!"

Ryuji Dressed Up

With a coat the color of baked bread, Ryuji has the most beautiful outfit in the world. Accessorize with a scarf and hat for instant foxiness to rival any silver fox.

Note the satisfied grin under that birthday-present cap.

Ryuji's Toys

He is already a grown dog, but his love for toys is the same as when he was a puppy.
Basically, he's the type who takes great pleasure in destroing things—only his beloved "blankie"
appears to be the exception. Other fabric things are chewed up before you know it.

His favorite rhino stuffed toy goes along with him for walks

44

"Hey tiger, come and play!"

"Hello pretty peonies! Happy to see you again."

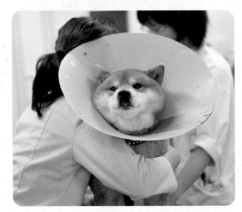

"Help, I hate going to the vet . . . even if, when there,
I'm surrounded by ladies, which I quite like!"

"One needs a collar at the beauty parlor too you know!"

"So can I eat it, can I, huh?!"

(Eagerly anticipating his favorite dish: Butch dog food. Note the tongue!)

"You *have* taken out the wasabi, haven't you?"

"Don't suppose you could spare just a mouthful of that meat?"

Walks with Ryuji

Ryuji just loves going for walks—even in inclement weather. At the local park, he always looks through the fence for any children playing with a ball—one of his favorite pastimes. Yet another day approached in a positive way, looking for fun.

Ryuji has a stubborn streak a mile wide. If something captures his attention he'll often come to a sudden halt. The only thing to do is tug on the lead and try to make him move forward, though it's hard to suppress a smile at that look pleading, "Please don't make me go!"

54

Outings with Ryuji

Ryuji dislikes long car trips, so we don't go too far. That said, he does love a good outing, seemingly quite at ease, even in places he's never been before, quickly taking the lead.

He may hate being given a bath, but playing in rivers is another matter entirely. If the mood takes him, he'll even bravely plunge in quite deep water.

Outings with Ryuji

Ryuji on his first trip to the seaside.
Taken to the water's edge, he immediately
had a great time, splashing a lot.

Ryuji and the Seasons

Being with Ryuji makes me closer to the changing of the seasons. He shows me that there are lovely views where before I would never even have stopped to look. And he's also connected me to many events and people that I would never have encountered otherwise.

"Mmm, you smell nice."

"A big hello to Bibi, my little porcine pal!"

"Sorry to keep you all waiting . . ."

"Little Pea, a sparrow we often encounter at a local café, waiting for bread scraps brought by my wife!"

"Right, I'm off ! Follow me!"

"Lovely to make your acquaintance, ma'am!"

"A good dog, yep, that's me. Heh heh."

"Watch out behind me there!"

"See this sweet, silky-soft pancake of a face?
DON'T TOUCH IT!"

"Oh come on, play with me. Play!"

"My regular pro-wrestling bout with a villager friend!"

"Shall we dance?"

Ryuji at the Restaurant

The little restaurant run by Ryuji's "wife" has been here for over 30 years, and Ryuji serves not as a mascot but as a guard dog of sorts. Though not usually inside the restaurant, on days off he has the run of it with Yome.

88

Ryuji and Yome

Before Ryuji we had a dog in the house called Ryutaro, a sleek black crossbreed. One cold winter's morning, the wife found this wonderful guard dog had passed quietly away in his kennel.

The wife fell into a terrible funk. Urged by a villager to get a new guard dog, she looked at many dogs, but felt nothing for any of them. Then, when she saw Ryuji, a single glance was all it took—she had to have him.

She called him "Ryuji," the spelling of which also means "Ryutaro II" or "Ryutaro's successor." Yet the personalities of the two dogs are totally different. To stress Ryuji's unique individuality, she writes his name in hiragana, that is, without the Japanese character that means "second."

08 7/5
本嶋りゅうじくん

Ryuji jumps up for his lead, very excited by the prospect of a walk.

They say couples start to look alike, and from behind, people around the village would agree.

Ryuji just adores facial massages from his wife.
A glance at his face shows that it feels much nicer than just being stroked.

After being told by the vet "Ryuji thinks of you as his 'wife,'" the appellation stuck.

Every glance through the viewfinder finds the "happy couple."

The only time Ryuji moves slowly is when walking with Yome. He may run off as fast as he can if anyone else holds the lead. There is only one mistress in the world he truly cares for. And every time I see the pair of them through the viewfinder it strikes me that maybe Ryuji was put on this earth to meet his wife.

Afterword

Until I met Ryuji, to be honest I was not that interested in dogs. Let alone did I ever imagine that I would be friends with them. Then, inevitably I suppose, a series of heartbreaking things happened to me, this cool and detached individual.

It was at that time that a certain dog turned to me with a big goofy grin on his face. I couldn't believe my eyes, yet at the same time, sensed a very real, soul-soothing healing. That dog was, of course, Ryuji, our shiba inu. And that day marked the start of my career as a paparazzo, pursuing his every look.

You don't have to go far in this world to find painful events or sad news. Amid it all, meeting a companion capable of lighting up people's lives has to be the ultimate gift. I really hope that all the dogs with nowhere to go and all the people like I once was are blessed with that same opportunity.

Shiba Inu
Ryuji

Instagram ID ☞ @ryuji513

First English edition published In December 2020
by PIE International Inc.
2-32-4 Minami-Otsuka, Toshima-ku, Tokyo, Japan 170-0005
www.pie.co.jp/english
international@pie.co.jp

Author	Yukiko Motoshima
Original Japanese edition design	Narumi Noshiro
Editor	Yuka Tsutsui (PIE International)
English typesetting and cover design	Andrew Pothecary (itsumo music)
Production	Aki Ueda (Pont Cerise)

ISBN: 978-4-7562-5379-8

First printing in December 2020

Printed and bound in China